Apache Mesos
Basics

Table of Contents

Introduction

The use of Apache Mesos is on the rise. This is attributed to the fact that most companies are now operating in a distributed environment. Due to this, there is a need to control how the resources are being used by the various nodes in the distributed environment. Apache Mesos is good tools which can help one achieve this in the most effective way. One can use it to manage the various nodes in such an environment and isolate the various resources. Due to the efficiency it offers to businesses, most companies are now using Apache Mesos. This is why you need to familiarize yourself with how it works. This book is an excellent guide for you to understand how Apache Mesos works. Enjoy reading!

Chapter 1- Getting Started with Apache Mesos

What is Apache Mesas?

Apache Mesas is a fault-tolerant manager which works in a centralized manner. It was designed to be used in distributed computing environments for provision of resource isolation and management across the clusters of slave nodes. This is in contrast to what happens in virtualization. This is because the concept of virtualization works by splitting a single physical resource into a number of virtual resources.

Mesas works by joining multiple physical resources into a single virtual resource. Mesas schedule the memory and CPU resources in a cluster in the same way that the Linux kernel schedules the local resources. The following are the four major components which make up a Mesos cluster:

1. Zookeeper

    Apache Zookeeper refers to a centralized configuration manager which is used by distributed applications such as Mesos for the coordination of activities across a cluster. Mesos makes use of the Zookeeper for election of the leading master and for the slaves to join a cluster.

2. Mesas masters

A Mesas master refers to an instance of Mesos which is in control of a cluster. A cluster usually has multiple Mesos masters for provision of fault tolerance in case of a failure, and one of these is elected to act as the leading master.

3. Mesas Slaves

A Mesas slave refers to an instance of Mesas which provides resources to the cluster. They are usually the worker instances, which mean they are the tasks allocated to slaves by a Mesas master.

4. Frameworks

When used alone, Mesas will only provide the basic kernel layer of a cluster. It allows the other applications which are contained in the system to request the necessary resources so as to be able to perform tasks, but it does nothing itself.

This means that the frameworks work to bridge the gap between the applications and the Mesas layer. You can view them as higher level abstractions which can makes it launch applications to the cluster.

5. Chromos

This is a corn-like scheduler for a Mesas cluster. It is fault-tolerant. It can be used for scheduling jobs, receiving notifications about failure and completion, and triggering other dependent jobs.

6. Marathon

In Linux, this can be seen as the unit daemons or upstart, which is designed for the long-running applications. It can be used for starting, stopping, and scaling applications across a cluster.

Apache Mesas was originally developed at the University of California in Berkeley. It works between the operating system and the applications, making it easy for us to deploy applications in large-scale clustered environments in a more efficient manner.

Installing Apache Mesos

Mesos usually runs on Mac OS X 64 bit and Linux OS 64 bit. For you to build Mesas from its source, you should have GCC 4.8.1+ or Clang 3.5+. If you need to have full support for process isolation in Linux, then you must have kernel version 3.10 or a higher version. There are two ways that you can get the Apache Mesas distribution, namely tar ball or by cloning the repo. These two methods are both supported, but you have to run the scripts differently in each.

Begin by downloading the latest and stable release of Apache Mesos from Apache.

$ wget http://www.apache.org/dist/mesos/1.2.0/mesos-1.2.0.tar.gz

$ tar -zxf mesos-1.2.0.tar.gz

If you are an advanced user, you can run the following command as a way of cloning the Mesas git repository:

$ git clone https://git-wip-us.apache.org/repos/asf/mesos.git

For the users of Ubuntu 14.04, do the following. Begin by updating the packages:

$ sudo apt-get update

Run the following command to install a few utility tools which are needed:

$ sudo apt-get install -y tar wget git

Get the latest version of OpenJDK and install it:

$ sudo apt-get install -y openjdk-7-jdk

If you are building it from the git repository, then you have to install the auto tools by running the following command:

$ sudo apt-get install -y autoconf libtool

You can then install the rest of the Mesas dependencies by running the following command:

$ sudo apt-get -y install build-essential python-dev python-virtualenv libcurl4-nss-dev libsasl2-dev libsasl2-modules maven libapr1-dev libsvn-dev

For the users of Ubuntu 16.04, follow the instructions given below. Begin by updating the packages:

$ sudo apt-get update

Install some utility tools as follows;

$ sudo apt-get install -y tar wget git

Install the latest version of OpenJDK:

$ sudo apt-get install -y openjdk-8-jdk

If you are building it from the git repository, install the autotools by running the following command:

$ sudo apt-get install -y autoconf libtool

The rest of the Mesas dependencies can then be installed as follows:

$ sudo apt-get -y install build-essential python-dev python-virtualenv libcurl4-nss-dev libsasl2-dev libsasl2-modules maven libapr1-dev libsvn-dev zlib1g-dev

You will have setup Apache Mesas in your Linux system.

For the users of Mac OS X 10.10 (or Yosemite), Mac OS X 10.11 (or El Capitan), macOS 10.12 (or Sierra), the following instructions will help you setup Apache Mesos in your system. Install the utilities for the command line:

$ xcode-select –install

Homebrew will help us perform the installation. Install it by running the following command:

$ ruby -e "$(curl -fsSL https://raw.githubusercontent.com/Homebrew/install/master/install**)"**

Install Java by running the following command:

$ brew install Caskroom/cask/java

In the next steps, we will be installing the other libraries and the Python dependencies. The libraries can be installed as follows:

$ brew install wget git autoconf automake libtool subversion maven

The Python dependencies will be installed via pip as follows:

$ sudo easy_install pip

$ pip install virtualenv

For the users of Mac OS 10.12, you should do the following:

The system comes installed with svn and apr headers. This means that we have to get these headers from the brew installation. We should first use the brew so as to unlink the installed ones so that the brew ones can install properly. Run the following commands;

$ brew unlink subversion # (If it is already installed)
$ brew install subversion

You can then suppress the warning as follows:

$ ../configure CXXFLAGS=-Wno-deprecated-declarations

You will never see the warnings.

Windows

Mesos version 1.0.0 introduced an experimental support for the Windows operating system.

Building Mesas

For you to build Mesas in Windows, the following system requirements should be met:

1. Begin by installing the latest version of the Visual Studio Community 2015. Ensure that you have selected Common Tools for Visual C++ as well as Windows 10 SDK. Launch Visual Studio Community so as to complete its setup and configuration.

2. Install the CMake 3.6.3 or a later version. Avoid running CMake before you can finish the setup for Visual Studio Community.

3. Install the Gnu Patch 2.5.9-7 or a later version.

4. If you are building from git, ensure that you have the Windows-style line endings, that is, git config core.autocrlf true.

1. Ensure that you have no spaces in the build directory. Example, C:/Program Files (x86)/mesos is an example of an invalid build directory.

2. Install Python 2.6+ and the virtualenv, but these are optional. This only becomes a necessity for those who are developing Mesos on Windows.

The instructions for the stock Windows 10 and the Windows Server 2012 or a newer version are as follows:

First, launch the command prompt for vs2015 x64 Native Tool. To find this, just open vs2015 and look under the "tools" menu for the "visual studio command prompt." You can then change your directory to the working directory:

cd mesos

For those who are developing on Windows, it will be good for you to run the bootstrap. Administrator privileges will be required for you to do this. The command for running bootstrap should be as follows:

.\bootstrap.bat

Note that the command begins with a dot (.).

You can now generate the solution and then build:

.\support\windows-build.bat

The value for the "PreferredToolArchitecture" environment variable should now be set to "x64," Although we will not be doing this from the control panel, note that you can use it to set the value for this system wide. Just run the following command to set it via the command line:

SET PreferredToolArchitecture=x64

Now that you have generated a visual studio solution, the IDE can be used for opening the project and skipping the following step;

msbuild Mesos.sln /m

We can find "mesos-agent.exe" in the folder named

"<repository>\build\src."

Change your directory as follows:

cd src

New isolators are exposed by the Windows agent and these have to be used with the "—isolation" flag. For you to start, just point your agent to the working master by use of the zookeeper information or an IP address. The following command will help you achieve this:

mesos-agent.exe --master=<master> --work_dir=<work folder> --launcher_dir=<repository>\build\src

However, it is good for you to know that there is a limitation with this kind of installation. At this point, we are only capable of running the agent on Windows, but the Mesos master has to run on a Posix machine.

Chapter 2- Authentication and Authorization

Authentication

The aim of authentication in Apache Mesos is to ensure that only the authorized users interact with the Mesos cluster. The following are the three ways that Mesos can use authentication:

1. To require the frameworks to be authenticated so as to register with the master.

2. To require the agents to be authenticated so as to register with the master.

3. To require the operators to be authenticated so as to use many HTTP endpoints.

The authentication feature comes disabled by default. After this feature is enabled, one can choose to use the default module for authentication or a custom authentication module. The default one makes use of the Cyrus SASL library. SASL is a framework which allows two endpoints to authenticate each other by use of a number of methods. In Mesos, the CRAM-MD5 is the default method of authentication.

For authentication with this method, the entity has to provide a credential, which in most cases is a *principal* and a *secret*. The principal in this case refers to the entity while the secret will be used to verify whether the entity is who it claims to be. The principal is used as the primary form of authentication and authorization.

Configuring Authentication

Authentication has to be configured by specifying a number of command-line flags during the launch of the Mesas master and the agent processes.

Master

Here is an exploration of the necessary command-line arguments for the master:

1. --[no-]authenticate – if set to "true," only the authenticated frameworks will be allowed to register. If it is set to "false" (the default), the unauthenticated frameworks will also be allowed to register.

2. --[no-]authenticate_http_readonly- if this is set to "true," then authentication will be needed as to the HTTP requests to HTTP read only endpoints which support authentication. If it is set to "false," then the endpoints can be used with no need for authentication. Such endpoints can be used for modification of the state of clusters.

3. --[no-]authenticate_http_readwrite- If it is set to "true," authentication will be required to make the HTTP requests to read-write HTTP endpoints which support authentication. If it is set to "false" (the default), the endpoints can be used with no authentication. The Read-write endpoints are the ones which can be used for modification of a cluster state.

4. --[no-]authenticate agents- If this is set to "true," only the authenticated agents will be allowed to register. If it is set to "false" (the default), unauthenticated agents will also be allowed to register.

5. - –authenticators- Specifies the authenticator module to be used. The default is the "crammd5," but more modules can be added by use of the --modules option.

6. --http_authenticators- Specifies the HTTP authenticator module to be used. The default is the basic (basic HTTP authentication), but you can add other modules by use of the --modules option.

7. --credentials – specifies the path to a text file having the list of the accepted credentials. It can be optional based on the authenticator which is being used.

Agent

1. --authenticate – specifies the module to be used. Defaults to crammd5.

2. --credential – similar to master's --credentials option but only one credential will be allowed. The credential will be used for identification of the agent to master.

3. --[no-]authenticate_http_readonly - If this is set to true, authentication will be required to make the HTTP requests to read-only HTTP endpoints which support authentication. If it is set to false (the default), the endpoints can be used with no authentication. Read-only endpoints are the ones that cannot be used for modification of the agent state.

4. --[no-]authenticate_http_readwrite – If it is set to true, authentication will be required to make the HTTP requests to read-write HTTP endpoints which support authentication. If it is set to false (the default), the endpoints will be used with no authentication.

5. --http_authenticators - Specifies the HTTP authenticator module to be used. The default is the "basic," but you can use the "—modules" option to add other modules.

6. --http_credentials – specifies the path leading to a text file with the list (in JSON format) of the accepted credentials. It can be optional, based on the authenticator which is being used.

An Example of CRAM-MD5

Create the credentials file for the master with the contents given below:

```
{
  "credentials" : [
   {
    "principal": "principal1",
    "secret": "secret1"
   },
   {
    "principal": "principal2",
    "secret": "secret2"
   }
  ]
}
```

Let us assume that you have saved the above file at "/home/user/credentials." You can then use the master to start the credentials file as shown below:

```
./bin/mesos-master.sh --ip=127.0.0.1 --
work_dir=/var/lib/mesos --authenticate --
authenticate_agents --
credentials=/home/user/credentials
```

Create another file, that is, "/home/user/agent_credential" and add a single credential in it as shown below:

```
{
  "principal": "principal1",
  "secret": "secret1"
}
```

You can then use the following command so as to start the agent:

./bin/mesos-agent.sh --master=127.0.0.1:5050 --credential=/home/user/agent_credential

The new agent should have run through the authentication with the master successfully. Mesos provides you with a number of test frameworks which you can use so as to test whether your authentication framework is running as expected or not. This is demonstrated below:

MESOS_AUTHENTICATE=true DEFAULT_PRINCIPAL=principal2 DEFAULT_SECRET=secret2 ./src/test-framework --master=127.0.0.1:5050

That is it!

Authorization

In Mesos, the purpose of authorization is to allow the operator to configure the actions which a certain principal will be allowed to perform. A good example is when the operator wants to configure the principal "X" to be able to register frameworks in the role "Y," but no other principal will be allowed to register a framework in any other role.

The "local authorizer" is used to provide the basic security in most cases. It is configured by use of Access Control Lists (ACLs). The local authorizer is normally used when the

--authorizer's flag has not been specified. The ACLs are normally specified by use of the ---acts flag. Let us discuss how one can implement both the local authorizer and the custom authorizer.

Local Authorizer

Roles vs. Principal

A principal is used to identify an entity that is interacting with Mesos. The role is used for the purpose of associating the resources with frameworks in a number of ways. This can be compared to what happens in UNIX. The principals can be seen as the usernames, while the roles can be seen as the groups.

ACLs

During the authorization of an action, the local authorizer has to go through a number of rules until when it finds a rule which either grants the subject permission or denies it the requested permission. In the case of the local authorizer, the rules are configured by use of access control lists (ACLs).

Each ACL is made up of an array of JSON objects, with each JSON object having two entries. The first entry is the principal describing the subject in need of performing the action and it is common to all the actions.

The second entry is determined by the action, and it describes the object we need to execute the action on. We also have the authorizable actions, which are the actions a subject can be granted to do. Examples of such actions include register_frameworks, run_tasts, reserve_resources, teardown_frameworks, etc.

Examples

Consider the following ACL. Only the "foo" principal is capable of registering frameworks to the "analytics" role. All principals are able to register themselves to any other role including the foo. This should be as follows:

```
{
 "register_frameworks": [
              {
                "principals": {
                  "values": ["foo"]
                },
                "roles": {
                  "values": ["analytics"]
                }
              },
              {
                "principals": {
                  "type": "NONE"
                },
                "roles": {
                  "values": ["analytics"]
```

```
            }
          }
        ]
}
```

That is how the ACL can be written. Consider this example. The "foo" principal is allowed to register frameworks with "analytics" and "ads" roles, but not with any other role. Any other principal is capable of registering frameworks with any other role. This should be as follows:

```
{
  "register_frameworks": [
              {
                "principals": {
                  "values": ["foo"]
                },
                "roles": {
                  "values": ["analytics", "ads"]
                }
              },
              {
                "principals": {
                  "values": ["foo"]
                },
                "roles": {
                  "type": "NONE"
                }
              }
```

```
        ]
}
```

Consider the next example. Only the "foo" principal is allowed to register frameworks with "analytics" role. All the other frameworks are allowed to register the frameworks with any other role. This can be expressed as follows:

```
{
  "register_frameworks": [
          {
            "principals": {
              "values": ["foo"]
            },
            "roles": {
              "values": ["analytics"]
            }
          },
          {
            "principals": {
              "type": "NONE"
            },
            "roles": {
              "values": ["analytics"]
            }
          }
          ]
}
```

Here is the next example. The "foo" principal is allowed to register frameworks with the "analytics" role, but not with any other role. No other principal will be allowed to register frameworks with any role, including the *. This can be expressed as follows:

```
{
  "permissive": false,
  "register_frameworks": [
              {
                "principals": {
                  "values": ["foo"]
                },
                "roles": {
                  "values": ["analytics"]
                }
              }
            ]
}
```

In the example given below, the "permissive" has been set to false, meaning that the principals will only be able to run tasks as the users of the operating system "guest" or "bar," but not as any other users:

```
{
  "permissive": false,
  "run_tasks": [
          {
              "principals": { "type": "ANY" },
```

```
        "users": { "values": ["guest", "bar"] }
    }
    ]
}
```

In the next example, the "foo" and "bar" principals are able to run the tasks as agent operating systems user names "alice" but not any other user. There is no other principal allowed to run tasks:

```
{
  "permissive": false,
  "run_tasks": [
        {
          "principals": { "values": ["foo", "bar"] },
          "users": { "values": ["alice"] }
        }
    ]
}
```

In this example, only the "foo" principal will be able to run tasks as agent operating system user "guest" but not other user. Any other principal or a framework with no principal will be able to run the tasks as any other user. This is shown below:

```
{
  "run_tasks": [
        {
          "principals": { "values": ["foo"] },
          "users": { "values": ["guest"] }
```

```
    },
    {
      "principals": { "values": ["foo"] },
      "users": { "type": "NONE" }
    }
    ]
}
```

No principal will be able to run tasks as agent operating system user "root" and any principal or a framework with no principal will be able to run tasks as any user. This should be as follows:

```
{
  "run_tasks": [
      {
        "principals": { "type": "NONE" },
        "users": { "values": ["root"] }
      }
      ]
}
```

Note that the order for definition of the various rules is very important.

Implementation of an Authorizer

You may be planning on implementing your own authorizer module. The authorization interface comes with three parts:

The "authorization::Request" probuf message is used to represent the request which is to be authorized. This follows the pattern of Subject-Verb-Object. The subject is the principal who is attempting to perform an action on an object.

The interface "Future<bool> mesos: Authorizer: authorized (const mesos:: authorization::Request& request)" is used to define the entry point for the authorizer modules. The call to the "authorized90" function will return a future which indicates the result of the authorization operation. In case the future is set to a "true," the authorization of the request was successful and if false, then the request was rejected.

The definition of an "authorization::Request" message has to be done in authorizer.proto as shown below:

```
message Request {
  optional Subject subject = 1;
  optional Action  action  = 2;
  optional Object  object  = 3;
}
message Subject {
  optional string value = 1;
}
message Object {
  optional string value = 1;
  optional FrameworkInfo framework_info = 2;
  optional Task task = 3;
  optional TaskInfo task_info = 4;
```

```
 optional ExecutorInfo executor_info = 5;
}
```

The fields "Subject" and "Object" are optional and if you don't set them, they will match an ACL only with ANY or NONE in their corresponding location. The Object has a number of fields and based on the action in use, one or more of the fields have to be set. An example is the "view_executors" which expects "framework_info" and "executor_info" to be set.

The "action" field of a "Request" message is just an enum. It is optional, but a valid action becomes necessary for each request as it will allow for backward compatibility during the addition of new fields.

For an efficient authorization of large objects and the multiple objects, a user may request the ObjectApprover via the "Future<Owned<ObjectApprover>> getObjectApprover(const authorization::Subject& subject, const authorization::Action& action)".

The OBjectApprover which results will give a "Try<bool> approved (const ObjectApprover::Object& object)" to check whether the objects are authorized. The "ObjectApprover::Object" normally follows the structure of "Request::Object" given previously. This is shown below:

struct Object
```
{
```

```cpp
    const std::string* value;
    const FrameworkInfo* framework_info;
    const Task* task;
    const TaskInfo* task_info;
    const ExecutorInfo* executor_info;
};
```

Since the fields are taking a pointer to every entity, ObjectApprover::Object needs no object to be copied.

Chapter 3- Container Image Support in Mesos Containerizer

There are several containerize which are supported in Mesos, including the Mesas Containerize and the Dockers containerize. The Mesos containerizer makes use of the native OS features directly so as to provide isolation between the containers, while the Dockers containerize delegates the container management to the Docker engine.

To support the container images, a new component was introduced in Mesas containerize, and this was named image provisioned. The image provisioned is responsible for caching, pulling, and preparing the container root file systems. Also, it extracts the runtime configurations from the container images that will in turn be passed to the corresponding isolators for a proper isolation. Currently, the Ducker and APPC images are supported.

Configuring the Agent

For container image support to be enabled in the Mesas containerize, the operator has to specify the

"--image_providers" agent flag that tells the Mesos containerizer the types of the container images which are allowed.

A number of isolators should be turned on so as to provide a proper isolation depending on runtime configurations which have been specified in the container image. The operator should add the isolators given below to the "—isolation" flag:

- filesystem/linux: The support for the container images involves a change to the filesystem root, and only the filesystem/linux currently supports this, hence the need for this isolator. This isolator requires a root permission.

- docker/runtime: We use this to provide support for the runtime configurations as specified in the Docker images (example, Entrypoint/Cmd, and environment variables). Note that if you fail to specify this isolator and the "--image_providers" has Docker, then the agent will fail to start.

To summarize this, if you need to enable the support for container image in the Mesos containerizer, you have to specify the flags given below:

**$ sudo mesos-agent **
  **--containerizers=mesos **
  **--image_providers=appc,docker **
  --isolation=filesystem/linux,docker/runtime

Framework API

The "Image" probuf message was introduced so as to allow the container images to be able to specify container images for containers. There are two types, which are "APPC" and "DOCKER," which represent the Appc and Dockers images.

For the Docker images, "name" refers to the Docker image reference in the [REGISTRY_HOST[:REGISTRY_PORT]/]REPOSITORY[:TAG|@DIGEST].

```
message Image {
 enum Type {
  APPC = 1;
  DOCKER = 2;
 }

  message Appc {
   required string name = 1;
   optional Labels labels = 3;
  }

  message Docker {
   required string name = 1;
  }
```

```
required Type type = 1;

// Only 1 of the image messages given below should be set
so as to match
// the type.
optional Appc appc = 2;
optional Docker docker = 3;
}
```

The framework should specify "MesosInfo" in the "ContainerInfo" so as to launch the containers with the container images. This means that the framework should set the type to the "ContainerInfo.MESOS," which should indicate that it needs to use Mesos containerizer. If the "MesosInfo.image" isn't specified, our container will use host filesystem. If the "MesosInfo.image" is specified, then this will be used as the container image during the launch of the container.

Testing

First, begin by starting the Mesos master. The following command will help you do this:

sudo sbin/mesos-master --work_dir=/tmp/mesos/master

Launch the Mesas agent as follows:
**$ sudo GLOG_v=1 sbin/mesos-agent **

```
--master=<MASTER_IP>:5050 \
--isolation=docker/runtime,filesystem/linux \
--work_dir=/tmp/mesos/agent \
--image_providers=docker \
--executor_environment_variables="{}"
```

You can now go ahead and make use of the Mesos CLI, that is, mesos-execute so as to launch the Docker container. The "--shell=false" will tell Mesos to make use of the default entrypoint and cmd which have been specified in Docker image. This is shown below:

```
$ sudo bin/mesos-execute \
  --master=<MASTER_IP>:5050 \
  --name=test \
  --docker_image=library/redis \
  --shell=false
```

We now need to verify whether our container is running or not. You just have to launch the redis client as follows:

```
$ sudo docker run -ti --net=host redis redis-cli
127.0.0.1:6379> ping
PONG
127.0.0.1:6379>
```

Chapter 4- Task Health Checking

In some situations, applications may misbehave, crash, or fail to respond. This calls for a way to help us recover from such situations. Some frameworks such as Marathon and Apache Aurora come with their own logic, which helps them check on the health of their tasks.

For this to be done, the framework scheduler has to send a ping request such as via HTTP to the host in which the task is running, and then an arrangement is made for the executor or task to respond to the ping. However, this is associated with a number of problems because of the way that Mesos operates.

To solve the problems, the latest versions of Mesos has introduced the Mesos-native health check which helps in definition of a common API for the HTTP(S), command, and TCP health checks, and a reference implementation is provided for all the built-in executors. Let us discuss some of the health checks supported in Apache Mesos.

Mesos-native Health Checks

This type of check usually runs on the node. The executor is responsible for performing the checks, but not the scheduler. With this, the scalability usually improves, but the task of detecting faults which occur outside becomes a challenge.

The task status updates have been leveraged so as to transfer health check status to the Mesos master and then further to the scheduler of the framework in a bid to ensure an "at-least-once" delivery guarantee. The "healthy" Boolean field is used for conveying the health status, but in some cases, this may become insufficient. This indicates a task which has failed health checks will be in RUNNING with the "healthy" set to "false."

Once a task has turned unhealthy, the task status update message with "healthy" field which is set to a "false" will be sent to Mesos master and then forwarded to the scheduler. The executor should kill the task once the number of the consecutive failures which have been defined in "consecutive_failures" field of "HealthCheck protobuf" has been reached.

Command Health Checks

These types of health checks are described by "CommandInfo" protobuf, with some fields being ignored, which are the "CommandInfo.user" and "CommandInfo.uris." It works by specifying a command which will be used for validation of the health of the task. The executor will then launch the command and check for its status. A 0 is seen as a success, and any other status is treated as a failure.

If you need to specify a command health check, the "type" has to be set to "HealthCheck::COMMAND" and then populate the CommandInfo as shown below:

```
HealthCheck healthCheck;
healthCheck.set_type(HealthCheck::COMMAND);

healthCheck.mutable_command()->set_value("ls
/checkfile > /dev/null");

task.mutable_health_check()->CopyFrom(healthCheck);
```

HTTP(S) Health Checks

These checks are described by the "HealthCheck.HTTPCheckInfo" protobuf with the scheme, path, port, and statuses fields. The "curl" command is normally used for sending a "GET" request to the "scheme://<host>:port/path." The parameter <host> has not been configured, and it will be resolved automatically to 127.0.0.1. The field for "scheme" can only support "http" and "https" values only. The field for "port" has to specify the port on which the task is listening, but not a mapped one.

For you to specify a HTTP health check, you should set type to a "HealthCheck::HTTP" and then populate the HTTPCheckInfo as shown in the following example:

```
HealthCheck healthCheck;
healthCheck.set_type(HealthCheck::HTTP);
healthCheck.mutable_http()->set_port(8080);
healthCheck.mutable_http()->set_scheme("http");
healthCheck.mutable_http()->set_path("/health");
task.mutable_health_check()->CopyFrom(healthCheck);
```

TCP Health Checks

These types of checks are described by "HealthCheck.TCPCheckInfo" protobuf which contains a single field for "port" and this has to specify the actual port on which the task is listening as opposed to a mapped port. To probe the task, we use the "mesos-tcp-connect" command of Mesos, which will try to establish a HTTP connection to "<host>:port."

If it is possible for a connection to be established, the health check will then be considered to be successful.

If it is necessary, the executors have to enter the network namespace of the task prior to launching of the "mesos-tcp-connect" command. To specify the TCP health check, just set the "type" to "HealthCheck::TCP" and then populate the "TCPCheckInfo" as shown in the example given below:

```
HealthCheck healthCheck;
healthCheck.set_type(HealthCheck::TCP);
healthCheck.mutable_tcp()->set_port(8080);

task.mutable_health_check()->CopyFrom(healthCheck);
```

The HealthCheck protobuf has common options which control how a health check can be interpreted by the executor. Examples of these options include the following:

1. delay_seconds- this specifies the amount of time you have to wait for you to start health checking the task.

2. interval_seconds- refers to the interval between the health checks.

3. consecutive_failures- refers to the number of the consecutive failures until a task is killed by the executor.

4. timeout_seconds- the amount of time we wait for a health check to complete. Once this timeout expires, the health check will be aborted and then treated as a failure.

Example:

In the following, we have some code which specifies a Docker container having a simple HTTP server which is listening on the port 8080 and HTTP Health check which will be performed after each second beginning from the task launch, allowing consecutive failures during the first 15 seconds and a response time under a 1 second. Here is the code:

TaskInfo task = createTask(...);

// Use Netcat for emulation of an HTTP server.
const string command =

```
    "nc -lk -p 8080 -e echo -e \"HTTP/1.1 200
OK\r\nContent-Length: 0\r\n\"";

task.mutable_command()->set_value(command)


Image image;
image.set_type(Image::DOCKER);
image.mutable_docker()->set_name("alpine");


ContainerInfo* container = task.mutable_container();
container->set_type(ContainerInfo::MESOS);
container->mutable_mesos()->mutable_image()-
>CopyFrom(image);

// Set the `grace_period_seconds` since it will take
// sometime before launching of Netcat to serve the
requests.

HealthCheck healthCheck;
healthCheck.set_type(HealthCheck::HTTP);
healthCheck.mutable_http()->set_port(8080);
healthCheck.set_delay_seconds(0);
healthCheck.set_interval_seconds(1);
healthCheck.set_timeout_seconds(1);
healthCheck.set_grace_period_seconds(15);
task.mutable_health_check()->CopyFrom(healthCheck);
```

All built-in executors depend on a health check library which resides in "src/checks," An executor usually creates an instance of HealthChecker for each task and passes the health check definition and the extra parameters. In return to this, the library will notify the executor of the changes in the health status of the task.

Chapter 5- Framework Rate Limiting

This feature aims at protecting the throughput of a high-SLA (such as production, service, etc) frameworks in a multi-framework environment by having the master throttle messages from the other (example, development, batch) frameworks.

To throttle the messages from framework, Mesos cluster operator usually sets qps (queries per seconds) for every framework which is identified by a principal. The master promises not to process the messages from the framework at a rate which is above qps. After that, the outstanding messages are then kept in the memory on the master.

Configuration of Rate Limits

The following code shows a sample config file (in the JSON format) which can be specified with the "--rate_limits" master flag. Here it is:

```
{
  "limits": [
    {
      "principal": "foo",
      "qps": 55.5
      "capacity": 100000
    },
```

```json
{
  "principal": "bar",
  "qps": 300
},
{
  "principal": "baz",
}
],
"aggregate_default_qps": 333,
"aggregate_default_capacity": 1000000
}
```

In the above example, the framework "foo" has been throttled at configured qps and capacity. The framework "bar" has been given unlimited capacity, and the framework "baz" has not been throttled at all. In case there is a fourth framework "qux," or if there is a framework with no principal connected to a master, it will be throttled by rules "aggregate_default_qps" and the "aggregate_default_capacity."The JSON configuration is made up of the following fields:

1. Principal- this field must be provided, and it identifies the entity which is being throttled or explicitly being given the unlimited rate. It has to match the "FrameworkInfo.principal:" of the framework. Note that it is possible for you to have a number of networks which make use of the same principal, and the traffic which emanates

from these networks will be throttled at a QPS which is specified.

2. qps- this is queries per second or the rate, and it is optional. Once it has been set, the master will guarantee that it will not process the messages from the principal which is higher than the rate. However, it is possible for the master to be slower than the rate, especially in cases where too high a rate has been specified.

3. capacity- this is optional. The number of the OUTSTANDING messages frameworks of the principal may be put on a master. If it is not specified, the principal will be given an unlimited capacity. The queued messages may use too much of the memory and make the master OOM in case the capacity has been set too high or it has not been set.

The rate and the limit represent an aggregate for all, meaning that their combined traffic has been throttled together. If you fail to specify the "aggregate_default_qps," then the "aggregate_default_capacity" will be ignored. Again, if the above fields are not specified, then the frameworks which are unspecified will not be throttled. This gives you an unlimited way to give the frameworks an unlimited rate.

Chapter 6- Building an Apache Mesos Framework

In this chapter, we will help you understand how to build your own Apache Mesas framework. The reason for doing this is that we need you to exercise control when running Apache Mesas. A good example is when you are in business. It is possible for you to create a framework which will help you to prioritize the tasks which should give the highest returns.

We have one elected master which tracks the resources on the slaves and offers the resources to the frameworks. Frameworks are able to take the offers and then use this for launching a task on slaves. The tasks are run on the executor, which is a built-in Command Executor responsible for managing the task on our behalf on the machine. The framework can be seen as a scheduler.

In this case, we will be writing our own minimal framework and an executor. In Mesos, communication is done by the use of protocol buffers, and there are many language binders. We will use the Java programming language.

Registration of the Framework

The first thing a Mesos framework is expected to do is registering itself with the elected Mesos master so as to start receiving the resource offers. The offers should end up in scheduler implementation.

In Java, it is possible for us to use the MesosSchedulerDriver so to take care of the wiring on our behalf. We set our new MesosSchedulerDriver up simply by passing in some reference to the scheduler and telling it everything needed to know so as to communicate and then register with the Mesos master. The following code will help us achieve this:

```
private static void runFramework(String mesosMaster) {
        Scheduler scheduler = new
ExampleScheduler(getExecutorInfo());

        MesosSchedulerDriver driver = new
MesosSchedulerDriver(scheduler,

                        getFrameworkInfo(),
mesosMaster);

        int status = driver.run() ==
Protos.Status.DRIVER_STOPPED ? 0 : 1;

        driver.stop();
        System.exit(status);
}
```

Launching the Tasks

The "ExampleScheduler" has been used to implement the interface org.apache.mesos.Scheduler. The "resourceOffers" method forms the key of the scheduler, as it allows us to process the incoming offers from the Mesos and then use them so as to launch tasks. For a demonstration, we will just be taking any offer which we get as shown below:

```java
public void resourceOffers(SchedulerDriver
schedulerDriver, List offers) {


    for (Protos.Offer offer : offers) {
        Protos.TaskID taskId =
buildNewTaskID();


        Protos.TaskInfo task =
Protos.TaskInfo.newBuilder()

                .setName("task " +
taskId).setTaskId(taskId)
                .setSlaveId(offer.getSlaveId())

    .addResources(buildResource("cpus", 1))

    .addResources(buildResource("mem", 128))


    .setData(ByteString.copyFromUtf8("" +
taskIdCounter))

    .setExecutor(Protos.ExecutorInfo.newBuilder(exe
cutorInfo))
                .build();
        launchTask(schedulerDriver, offer, task);
    }
}
```

For us to launch a Task, Mesos has to be informed of the offers which we should take and how our Task should be configured. It is possible for us to take the majority of Task settings from an offer, but in a real framework, we should first look at the resources which we are offered and then adjust the configuration of the tasks accordingly. It is also possible for us to pass in data, and this will be delivered to the executor. This is a benefit of writing our own executor rather than relying on a default one. Messages can be sent between our framework and the executor.

The Executor

The executor components and the framework are loosely coupled. Since we are demonstrating this, we have kept them in a single project. The executor is expected to implement the interface org.apache.mesos.Executor, and the most important function in this case will be the launchTask. This is shown below:

```
public void launchTask(ExecutorDriver executorDriver,
Protos.TaskInfo taskInfo) {


        Integer id =
Integer.parseInt(taskInfo.getData().toStringUtf8());

        String reply = id.toString();

        executorDriver.sendFrameworkMessage(reply.get
Bytes());

        Protos.TaskStatus status =
Protos.TaskStatus.newBuilder()
```

```
        .setTaskId(taskInfo.getTaskId())

        .setState(Protos.TaskState.TASK_FINISHED).buil
d();

        executorDriver.sendStatusUpdate(status);
}
```

In the above example, we have taken the data which is being passed from the scheduler which has then been pinged back to the framework. Mesos has also been informed that the task was successfully completed. If this was in a real environment, we would have to launch some programs or tasks, wait for them to complete, and then send any appropriate messages regarding the status.

Chapter 7- Maintenance Primitives

Operators are in need of performing maintenance tasks on the machines which make up a Mesos cluster. Most upgrades in Mesas can be done without having to disrupt any running tasks, but in some tasks, these have to be disrupted. Examples of such circumstances include the following:

- Hardware repair
- Kernel upgrades
- Agent upgrades

Frameworks need visibility into the actions which disrupt the cluster operation so as to meet the Service Level Agreements or we have to ensure uninterrupted services to the end users.

Scheduling maintenance

A machine is usually transitioned from the Up mode to the Draining mode once it is scheduled for maintenance. To transition your machine into the Draining mode, the operator has to construct a maintenance schedule like a JSON document and the posts it to /maintenance/schedule HTTP endpoint on a Mesos master.

In a production environment, the schedule has to be constructed in such a way that there are enough operational agents at any point in time so that there can be uninterrupted service by frameworks.

A good example is when you have a cluster made up of three machines; two machines can be scheduled for an hour of maintenance, and an hour for your last machine. The unavailability timestamps should be expressed in nanoseconds, just like the UNIX epoch.

The schedule can now be as follows:

```
{
  "windows" : [
   {
     "machine_ids" : [
      { "hostname" : "machine1", "ip" : "10.0.0.1" },
      { "hostname" : "machine2", "ip" : "10.0.0.2" }
     ],
     "unavailability" : {
      "start" : { "nanoseconds" : 1443830400000000000 },
      "duration" : { "nanoseconds" : 3600000000000 }
     }
   }, {
     "machine_ids" : [
      { "hostname" : "machine3", "ip" : "10.0.0.3" }
     ],
```

```
    "unavailability" : {
    "start" : { "nanoseconds" : 1443834000000000000 },
    "duration" : { "nanoseconds" : 3600000000000 }
    }
   }
  ]
}
```

The operator can now post a schedule to the /maintenance/schedule
endpoint of the master. This is demonstrated below:

```
curl http://localhost:5050/maintenance/schedule \
  -H "Content-type: application/json" \
  -X POST \
  -d @schedule.json
```

The machines which are on a maintenance schedule need not be
registered with the Mesos master at the time when the schedule is
being set. The operator can as well choose to add a machine to the
maintenance schedule during the time that an agent is being
launched into the machine. This is a good practice if one needs to
prevent a faulty machine from starting an agent during the boot
time.

Starting Maintenance

For the operator to start the maintenance, he has to post the list of machines to /machine/down HTTP endpoint. The JSON format is used for specification of the list of machines, and each element contained in the list is a MachineID.

A good example is when you need to start the maintenance in your two machines. This can be as follows:

```
[
  { "hostname" : "machine1", "ip" : "10.0.0.1" },
  { "hostname" : "machine2", "ip" : "10.0.0.2" }
]

curl http://localhost:5050/machine/down \
  -H "Content-type: application/json" \
  -X POST \
  -d @machines.json
```

The master will check at the machine list for the properties explained below:

1. The list of the machines should not be empty.

2. Every machine should only appear once.

3. Each of the machines should have the IP or host name included. Note that the hostname in this case is not case-sensitive.

4. In case the IP of the machine is included, it has to be correctly formed.

5. All the machines which are listed have to be listed in the schedule.

In case any two of the above properties fail to be met, then the operation will have to be rejected with a corresponding error message while the state of the master will remain unchanged.

The operator is capable of starting the maintenance on any machine which has been scheduled for maintenance. It is impossible for a machine which has not been scheduled for maintenance to be transitioned from the Up mode to the Down mode. However, it is possible for the operator to schedule the machine for maintenance by use of the timestamp which is equal to the current time or in past.

The endpoint can be used for the purpose of starting the maintenance on the machines which have not currently been registered with the Mesos master.

This is of great importance in cases where the machine has failed and the user needs to remove it from a cluster. If maintenance is started on the machine, then it will prevent the instance of accidentally rebooting the machine and getting it into the cluster.

The operator is expected to explicitly transition the machine from the Draining to the Deactivated mode. This means that Mesos will keep the machine in the Draining mode even after the passage or arrival of the unavailability window. This is an indication that the operation of the machine will not be interrupted in any way, and the offers for the machine will still be sent.

After the operator has triggered the maintenance, all the agents which are located in the machine will be instructed to shut down. The agents will then be removed from the master, meaning that the TASK_LOST status update will have to be sent for each task which is running in the agents. The "slaveLost" callback for the scheduler driver will be invoked for each of removed agents. Any machines located on the machine under maintenance will also be prevented from performing a re-registration with the master in the future. This will apply until the maintenance has been completed and the machine has been brought back up.

Completing Maintenance

After completion of the maintenance or if it needs to be cancelled, the operator is capable of stopping the maintenance. This process is similar to the starting of maintenance; the operator has to post the list of the machines to the /machine/up endpoint of the master.

```
[
  { "hostname" : "machine1", "ip" : "10.0.0.1" },
  { "hostname" : "machine2", "ip" : "10.0.0.2" }
]
```

```
curl http://localhost:5050/machine/up \
 -H "Content-type: application/json" \
 -X POST \
 -d @machines.json
```

The "unavailability" field of the maintenance schedule which indicates the duration of the maintenance window is a guess by the operator which requires some effort. You are allowed to stop the maintenance before the unavailability interval can end. Automatic transition of a machine out of maintenance is not possible.

Frameworks are usually informed about the cancellation or completion of maintenance once the offers from a machine begin to be sent.

Conclusion

We have come to the end of this guide. Apache Mesas is a software program which can be used for the management of computer clusters. It employs the concept of the Linux Croups so as to provide isolation for the memory, CPU, I/O, and the file system. The master daemon for Mesas is responsible for the management of agent daemons which run on cluster node, as well as the Mesas frameworks which run the tasks on the agents. The control of how the resources are used is the task of the master, and this is done by the giving of resource offers.

The master is the one tasked with the responsibility of determining the number of resources which are assigned to each cluster, which is determined by the policy used in the organization such as a strict policy or fair sharing. There is a need to maintain a wide range of policies which will determine how the resources are used. Due to this, the master has to come up with a modular approach which makes it possible for the addition of new allocation modules through the plugin mechanism. Each framework running on Mesas consists of a scheduler who is responsible for registration with the master which is to be offered resources and the executor process which will be started on the agent nodes for the framework to run the tasks.